HABITAT DAY

DESERT

BY BRENNA MALONEY

Children's Press®
An imprint of Scholastic Inc.

A special thank-you to the team at the Cincinnati Zoo & Botanical Garden for their expert consultation.

Library of Congress Cataloging-in-Publication Data available

ISBN 978-1-339-02072-3 (library binding) / ISBN 978-1-339-02073-0 (paperback)

10 9 8 7 6 5 4 3 2 1   24 25 26 27 28

Printed in China   62
First edition, 2024

Book design by Kay Petronio

Photos ©: cover bottom and throughout: Caglar Gungor/Dreamstime; back cover center left, 2 left: Mlenny/Getty Images; 4-5 background: cinoby/Getty Images; 6-7: Jim McMahon/Mapman ®; 12-13: kristianbell/Getty Images; 18-19: Rinus Baak/Dreamstime; 24-25: Barry Mansell/SuperStock/Alamy Images; 28-29: Bruno D'Amicis/Nature Picture Library/Alamy Images; 30 bottom right: Anton Petrus/Getty Images.

All other photos © Shutterstock.

CAMEL

JERBOA

CONTENTS

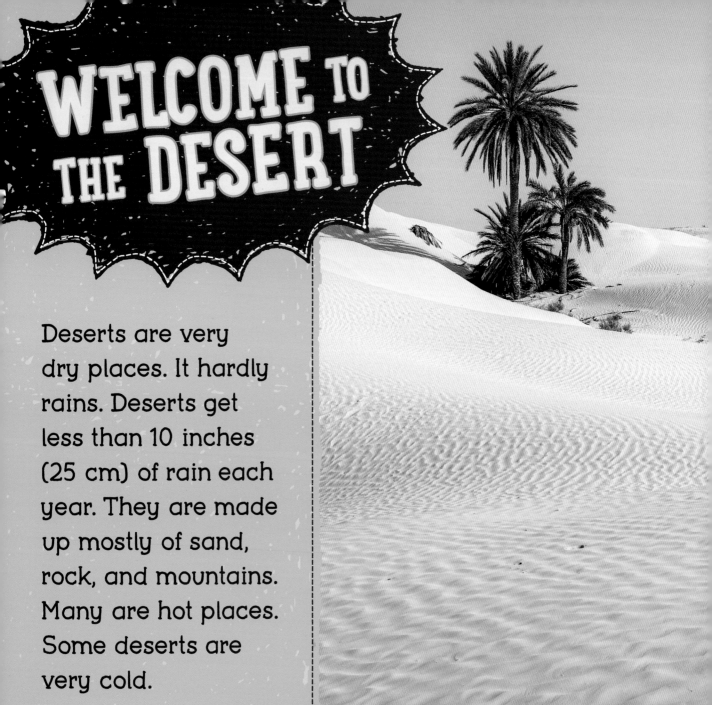

WELCOME TO THE DESERT

Deserts are very dry places. It hardly rains. Deserts get less than 10 inches (25 cm) of rain each year. They are made up mostly of sand, rock, and mountains. Many are hot places. Some deserts are very cold.

It may seem like nothing could live in a desert **habitat**. But many plants and animals, like the ones in this book, call the sandy desert home.

FACT Some desert animals **estivate** when it's too hot. They tunnel into the ground and rest until the temperature cools off.

WHERE IN THE WORLD?

Arctic

NORTH AMERICA

Mojave Desert

Tropic of Cancer

The **Mojave Desert** is in the United States. It holds the record for the highest air and surface temperatures on Earth.

Equator

PACIFIC OCEAN

ATLANTIC OCEAN

SOUTH AMERICA

Atacama Desert

Tropic of Capricorn

The driest desert on Earth is the **Atacama Desert** in South America. It receives less than 0.2 inches (5 mm) of rain each year.

The biggest desert in the world is **Antarctica!** It rarely rains or snows here. The dryness makes it a desert.

The Antarctica and Arctic deserts are mostly covered in ice. The other deserts are mostly covered in sand.

FACT

ARCTIC OCEAN

Arctic

Oleshky Sands

The **Oleshky Sands** in Ukraine is one of the largest deserts in Europe.

EUROPE

ASIA

Gobi Desert

The **Gobi Desert** in Asia has big temperature changes. It can change as much as 63°F (35°C) in the same day!

PACIFIC OCEAN

Sahara Desert

The **Sahara Desert** covers most of northern Africa. It has some of the largest sand dunes in the world.

INDIAN OCEAN

AFRICA

AUSTRALIA

Great Victoria Desert

The **Great Victoria Desert** is the largest in Australia.

Desert

SOUTHERN OCEAN

Antarctica

LIFE IN THE DESERT

The animals and plants that live in sandy deserts can all survive with **extreme** temperatures and little water. Plants, such as cactus, are usually small and have small leaves or spines. This helps them save water.

MEERKAT

BLACK-TAILED JACKRABBIT

CACTUS

SHOVEL-SNOUTED LIZARD

FENNEC FOX

JERBOA

CAMEL

SIDEWINDER

Many animals have light-colored fur to keep cool and protect their skin. Long eyelashes and furry faces keep sand and sun out of their eyes and ears. Some desert animals are **herbivores**. They eat plants. Others are **carnivores**. They eat meat. Some eat both.

DAYTIME

NIGHTTIME

The spikes on desert plants stop animals from eating them.

FACT

By day, the bright sun heats the desert sand. Temperatures can rise above 100°F (38°C). But the sand cannot hold this heat. Once the sun sets, the temperature drops. The ground becomes cooler at night. The sky is dark or lit by the moon and stars. What do animals do during the scorching days and freezing nights? Read on to find out!

MEERKAT

It is early morning in a desert in Africa. A group of meerkats wakes up. They have spent the chilly night together in underground **burrows**. Their search for food begins at dawn. Meerkats are **omnivores**. They eat fruit and vegetables as well as small animals. While eating, they must look out for **predators**. Meerkats dig safe places called bolt-holes. They can hide quickly if there is danger.

DAYTIME

FACT Dark rings around meerkats' eyes help protect them from the bright sun.

The shovel-snouted lizard can use its nose to dig a hole and hide from predators.

FACT

SHOVEL-SNOUTED LIZARD

The meerkats will soon seek shade. The African desert heat does not bother the shovel-snouted lizard, though. Here, the sun toasts the sand to a sizzling 160°F (71°C). This lizard has a special way to handle the heat. It does a dance. It lifts two feet off the sand to cool them for 10 seconds. Then it lifts the other two feet for 10 seconds. The dancing protects the lizard's feet as it searches for insects to eat.

CAMEL

A camel has no interest in eating a dancing lizard! Camels are herbivores. They are built to survive in the African desert. They have three sets of eyelids and two rows of eyelashes to keep sand out of their eyes. They can shut their nostrils during sandstorms. Pads of skin on their chests and knees keep them from getting burned by the sand. Their thick lips protect them while they eat thorny plants.

A camel can go a week or more without water.

This armadillo can also curl up to protect itself. Its body is covered in bony plates.

SCREAMING HAIRY ARMADILLO

Camels can't be startled by a screaming hairy armadillo. They don't live in the same desert. But if surprised or scared, this armadillo really screams! Most animals back away from them. This South American animal is left alone to search for food during the daytime heat. They dig in the loose, sandy soil for insects, rodents, or lizards. They get most of the water they need from plants that they eat.

19

BLACK-TAILED JACKRABBIT

The sun begins to set in a North American desert. Black-tailed jackrabbits wake up from their naps at dusk. They've escaped the hottest part of the day, but it's still hot outside. The skin on their large ears is very thin. Heat escapes from their ears and keeps them cool. Black-tailed jackrabbits eat almost constantly. Grasses, twigs, and the bark from woody plants are favorites. As they hop across the hot desert sands, their fur-covered feet are protected.

Their light silver-and-tan fur also keeps black-tailed jackrabbits cooler.

The sidewinder is FAST. It can slither up to 18 miles per hour (29 kph)!

SIDEWINDER

North American jackrabbits must look out for predators like sidewinders. At dusk, sidewinders are just beginning to wake up. The sand is no match for these **venomous** snakes. As their body moves over loose sand, they form the letter S. This special way of moving helps sidewinders climb sandy slopes without slipping. They can move quickly while chasing rodents, lizards, and birds to eat.

GHOST-FACED BAT

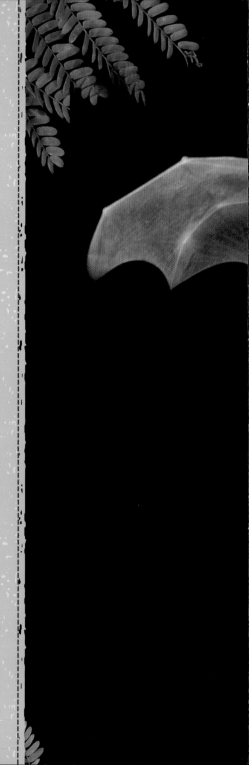

It is nighttime in a Central American desert. A flurry of fuzzy bodies takes to the skies. Ghost-faced bats leave their hot caves. They fly in fast-moving groups. These bats are strong fliers that feed on large moths. Little is known about these **nocturnal** creatures. They enter and leave their steamy caves several times while hunting. Ghost-faced bats may spend as many as seven hours each night searching for food.

FACT

Groups of ghost-faced bats can be as large as half a million bats!

Jerboas have large eyes to help them see well in the dark.

FACT

JERBOA

Night is no match for the jerboa. Jerboas are nocturnal. They spend most of the hot day in sandy underground burrows. During the cooler nights, they hunt for insects. This tiny rodent lives in deserts around the world. It can survive in the Sahara, the hottest desert. It can also survive in the Gobi Desert, one of the coldest. The jerboa has a mouse-like body, rabbity ears, and a pig-like snout. Its back legs are long and strong. It can jump really high to escape predators.

Pale fur **camouflages** fennec foxes against the sand. Camouflage protects them from predators.

FENNEC FOX

At night, fennec foxes use their large ears to listen for **prey** under the sand. When they hear a rodent or insect, they use all four paws to dig it out. Fennec foxes can survive in both African and Asian deserts. During the day, they rest. Their bat-like ears allow heat to escape their bodies, cooling them down. Panting also helps fennec foxes cool off when the temperature rises.

YOU DECIDE!

If you could choose, would you visit a sandy desert during the day or at night? The day brings bright sun and scorching heat. Don't forget your hat and sunscreen. The night brings darkness and freezing temperatures. You'll need your winter coat and a flashlight. Either way, deserts are always dry, so be sure to bring plenty of water! At home, you can learn even more about deserts and the amazing animals who live there!

GLOSSARY

burrow (BUR-oh) a tunnel or hole in the ground made or used as a home by a rabbit or other animal

camouflage (KAM-uh-flahzh) to disguise something so that it blends in with its surroundings

carnivore (KAHR-nuh-vor) an animal that eats meat

estivate (ES-tuh-vate) to spend a hot, dry season in an inactive state

extreme (ik-STREEM) very great

habitat (HAB-i-tat) the place where an animal or a plant is usually found

herbivore (HUR-buh-vor) an animal that eats plants

nocturnal (nahk-TUR-nuhl) active at night

omnivore (AHM-nuh-vor) an animal that eats both plants and meat

predator (PRED-uh-tur) an animal that lives by hunting other animals for food

prey (pray) an animal that is hunted by another animal for food

venomous (VEN-uhm-uhs) producing venom, or poison, that can pass to a victim through a bite or sting

INDEX

Page numbers in **bold** indicate images.

ABOUT THE AUTHOR

Brenna Maloney is the author of dozens of books. She lives and works in Washington, DC, with her husband and two sons. She wishes she had more pages to tell you about deserts. She can dance like a shovel-snouted lizard and holler like a screaming hairy armadillo, but she probably wouldn't last long in a desert without sunscreen.